IGCSE COMPUTER SCIENCE
150 PRACTICE QUESTIONS

VOLUME 1

H A Billinghurst

150 Practice Questions are not endorsed by Cambridge International. Please refer to the exam board specification to ensure that the full range of topics has been covered.

A CIP record of this book is available from the British Library

First printed August 2023

ISBN: 9798853786790

Independently published by Amazon KDP

To find out more about Holly Billinghurst and this book visit www.TeachAllAboutIT.uk

Other Books By This Author:

GCSE Computer Science 9-1 Complete Revision Visual Notes For OCR
GCSE Computer Science 9-1 Complete Revision Visual Notes For OCR
iGCSE Computer Science 9-1 Complete Revision Visual Notes
A Level Computer Science Complete Theory Revision Visual Notes For AQA
A Level Computer Science Complete Theory Revision Visual Notes For CIE

These questions cover the foundation topcis for iGCSE Computer Science and are linked to the lessons taught in year 1 of my iGCSE Computer Science Distance Learning course.

These are designed to be completed little and often and by completing just 5 questions each week, you'll be fully prepared for the exam without the stress of cramming!

The questions in this book can be used on their own, or in combination with my visual revision books and distance learning courses at

www.TeachAllAboutIt.uk

My name is Holly. and I'll be popping up throughout this book to help you.

Answers & guides to marking are available to access at the TeachAllAboutIt website

Set 1

1   Convert the binary number 01001001 to its denary value.

_____

_____

_____

_____   [1]

2   Convert the binary number 10000111 to its denary value.

_____

_____

_____

_____   [1]

3   Convert the binary number 10000111 to its denary value.

_____

_____

_____

_____   [1]

4   Give a suitable example of data to match each of the five data
    types:

String: _____

Char: _____

Integer _____

Real: _____

Boolean: _____   [5]

Command words are used in exam
questions to give you an idea of how to
answer.

The command word "give" suggests that
you just need to write the example without

5   Convert the denary number 165 to an 8 bit binary value.

_____

_____

_____

_____

_____   [1]

_____

Pause Point!

At the end of each set of questions, take a pause and check your answers.

Remember that "little & often" is much better at helping you revise than cramming all 150 questions at once!

Set 2

6 Hexadecimal is used for MAC addresses.
Give two other examples where hexadecimal can be used.

_____

_____

_____

_____

_____ [2]

7 Convert the denary number 151 to an 8 bit binary value.

_____

_____

_____

_____

_____ [1]

8 Convert the denary number 236 into hexadecimal. Show your working.

_____

_____

_____

_____

_____

_____ [2]

9 Using examples, explain why constants and variables are used in programming.

_____

_____

_____

_____

_____

_____ [4]

10 Convert the binary number 00011001 into hexadecimal.

_____

_____

_____

_____

_____ [1]

Pause Point!

When you're working on the number systems questions, keep an eye on the number of marks available.

If it's more than 1 mark, make sure that you're showing your working!

Set 3

11 Show how binary addition can be used to add these two numbers:
10110010 + 01100101

_____

_____

_____

_____

_____

_____

_____ [3]

12 Describe the need for both hexadecimal and denary in computer science.

_____

_____

_____

_____

_____

_____

_____ [4]

13 Convert the binary number 11001010 to its denary value.

_____

_____

_____

_____

_____ [1]

14 What is the name of the programming construct (building block) that is described as "the order in which the lines of code run"?

_____

_____

_____ [1]

15   A washing machine has a small display screen built into it.

One use of the display screen is to show an error code when a problem has occurred with a washing cycle.

The display screen shows a hexadecimal error code:

E04

This error code means that the water will not empty out of the washing machine. Convert this error code to binary.

_____
_____
_____
_____
_____
_____
_____
_____
_____   [3]

Pause Point!

When you're calculating hexadecimal numbers, present each digit as a 4 bit nibble of data.

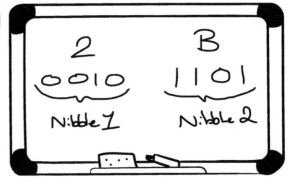

Set 4

16   Complete the blanks below to show how to convert the denary number -65 into a Two's Complement binary number.

	16	8		2	1

_____

_____

_____

_____   [2]

17   Complete the binary addition for 11101110 + 11000101.
Show your working in full.

_____

_____

_____

_____

_____   [3]

18   Describe the steps to convert a negative denary number into a Two's complement binary number.

_____

_____

_____

_____

_____

_____

_____   [4]

If you have a "describe" question, try using an example to structure your answer.

19   The following pseudocode algorithm uses nested IF statements.

```
IF Response = 1 THEN
  X ← X + Y
ELSE
  IF Response = 2 THEN
    X ← X – Y
  ELSE
    IF Response = 3 THEN
      X ← X * Y
    ELSE
      IF Response = 4 THEN
        X ← X / Y
      ELSE
        OUTPUT "No response"
      ENDIF
    ENDIF
  ENDIF
ENDIF
```

That's a lot of pseudocode!

Don't panic!

Break it down using a trace table so you can see what the code is doing.

Name the type of statement demonstrated by the use of IF ... THEN ... ELSE ... ENDIF

_____
_____
_____
_____   [1]

20   Convert the hexadecimal number 2CB into binary.

_____
_____
_____
_____
_____   [3]

Pause Point!

Set 5

21 Define the term "digital image" and explain the concept of a bitmap image.

_____
_____
_____
_____
_____
_____
_____   [4]

22 Calculate the size of an image with dimensions 800 pixels by 600 pixels and a color depth of 24 bits per pixel. Show all steps of the calculation.

_____
_____
_____
_____
_____
_____
_____   [4]

23 Describe the purpose of iteration in programming and provide an example of a programming construct used for iteration.

_____
_____
_____
_____
_____
_____
_____
_____
_____   [5]

24 List three common color depths used in digital images and explain the impact of color depth on image quality and file size.

_____

_____

_____

_____

_____

_____

_____

_____

_____

_____ [6]

25 Write a pseudocode algorithm to calculate the sum of all even numbers from 1 to 100.

_____

_____

_____

_____

_____

_____

_____

_____

_____

_____

_____

_____

_____ [7]

> **Pause Point!**

When you're writing a pseudocode algorithm, look at some of the examples used in the exam paper to remind you how to style your own code.

Set 6

26   Convert the decimal number 45 into a binary number.

_____

_____

_____

_____   [2]

27   Explain the difference between ASCII and Unicode character sets.

_____

_____

_____

_____

_____

_____   [3]

28   Write an algorithm that uses a sequence to print numbers from 1 to 10.

_____

_____

_____

_____

_____

_____   [2]

29   Write an algorithm that uses selection to print whether a number is even or odd.

_____

_____

_____

_____

_____

_____

_____

_____   [3]

30 Write an algorithm that uses iteration to print the first 5 multiples of a given number.

_____

_____

_____

_____

_____

_____

_____

_____

_____

_____

_____

_____

[3]

Pause Point!

$$x \leftarrow 100$$

OR

$$max\_num \leftarrow 100$$

Your pseudocode should use meaningful names.

Which of these two variables tells you what the data is for?

Set 7

31   Convert the positive decimal number 37 into an 8-bit binary
number using Two's Complement.

_____

_____

_____

_____

_____

_____

_____   [3]

32   Convert the negative decimal number -58 into an 8-bit binary
number using Two's Complement.

_____

_____

_____

_____

_____

_____   [3]

33   Perform the binary addition of 1101 (13 in decimal) and 1011 (11 in
decimal).

_____

_____

_____

_____

_____

_____

_____

_____

_____   [2]

Don't forget to show your
carried numbers & highlight the
overflow (*if there is any!*)

34 Explain how bit depth, samples, and sample rate contribute to the quality of digital sound.

_____

_____

_____

_____

_____

_____

_____

_____

_____

_____ [5]

35 Write an algorithm that uses sequence, selection, and iteration to find the sum of all even numbers in a given list.

_____

_____

_____

_____

_____

_____

_____

_____

_____

_____

_____

_____ [5]

Pause Point!

Sequence -

Selection -

Iteration

Set 8

36 (a) Explain the difference between serial and parallel data transmission. (b) Provide an example of a situation where each type of transmission would be most suitable.

_____

_____

_____

_____

_____

_____

_____

_____

_____

_____

_____   [4]

37 Define the terms simplex, duplex, and half-duplex in the context of data transmission.

Simplex: _____

_____

Duplex: _____

_____

Half-Duplex: _____

_____   [3]

38 Write a simple subroutine in either programming statements or pseudocode that calculates and returns the square of a number.

_____

_____

_____

_____

_____

_____   [3]

39   Explain the difference between lossless and lossy data compression.

_____
_____
_____
_____
_____
_____
_____ [2]

40   Provide an example of a situation where lossless compression would be preferred over lossy compression, and vice versa.

_____
_____
_____
_____
_____
_____
_____
_____
_____
_____
_____
_____ [4]

Pause Point!

Signposting is a way of making things really clear when writing your answers.

Using bullet points can help you make sure you've written enough.

Give Me Marks!

Set 9

41 Describe the process of Run Length Encoding with the help of an example.

_____

_____

_____

_____

_____

_____

_____

_____

_____ [3]

42 Explain the concept of Dictionary Encoding in data compression.

_____

_____

_____

_____

_____

_____ [2]

43 Draw a flowchart to represent a simple program that calculates the factorial of a number.

[3]

44 What are the key components of a flowchart?

_____

_____

_____

_____

_____

_____

_____

_____ [3]

45 Explain how different file types are suited to different types of data.

_____

_____

_____

_____

_____

_____

_____

_____

_____

_____

_____

_____ [3]

Pause Point!

RLE & Dictionary Encoding are both types of lossless compression. The choice depends on the data.

Set 10

46   Explain how a bitmap saves an image as a digital file.

_____

_____

_____

_____

_____

_____   [2]

47   How does the concept of 'colour depth' apply to digital images?

_____

_____

_____

_____

_____

_____   [2]

48   Describe the process of converting a negative decimal number to its two's complement binary representation.

_____

_____

_____

_____

_____

_____

_____   [3]

49   What is binary overflow and when does it occur?

_____

_____

_____

_____

_____   [2]

50   Describe the Fetch Decode Execute Cycle in a CPU.

_____

_____

_____

_____

_____

_____

_____

_____

_____

_____   [3]

Pause Point!

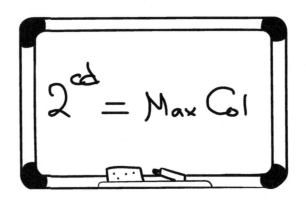

When you're working with bitmap images, the foruma above will help you to calculate colour depth and file sizes!

Set 11

51   What is the role of the following CPU registers: PC, MAR, MDR, CIR, Accumulator?

PC _____

MAR _____

MDR _____

CIR _____

Accumulator _____

_____   [5]

52   Explain the function of the following CPU components: ALU, CU, Cache.

ALU _____

_____

CU _____

_____

Cache _____

_____   [3]

53   Write a Python function that takes a 1D array as input and returns the sum of its elements.

_____

_____

_____

_____

_____

_____

_____

_____

_____

_____   [3]

54   Explain the concept of a subroutine in programming.

_____

_____

_____

_____

_____

_____   [2]

55   Write a Python subroutine that takes two arguments and returns their sum.

_____

_____

_____

_____

_____

_____

_____

_____

_____

_____

_____

_____

_____   [2]

Pause Point!

If a programming question asks you to use a subroutine, make sure that you include your code inside either a procedure or a function!

Set 12

56   Explain what an embedded system is and give two examples of where they are used.

_____
_____
_____
_____
_____
_____
_____
_____
_____   [3]

57   List three input devices and three output devices commonly used in a computer system.

Input 1 _____

Input 2 _____

Input 3 _____

Output 1 _____

Output 2 _____

Output 3 _____   [6]

58   Describe the role of sensors in control systems. Give two examples of such sensors.

_____
_____
_____
_____
_____
_____
_____
_____   [3]

59 Explain how digital characters are represented.

_____

_____

_____

_____

_____

_____

_____

_____ [3]

60 Describe the concept of positive and negative binary numbers using two's complement.

_____

_____

_____

_____

_____

_____ [3]

Pause Point!

The detail you need to know for Input/Output devices have reduced in this new specification - you still need to be able to identify a suitable device for a scenario...

Set 13

61 Explain the concept of binary addition with overflow using an example.

_____

_____

_____

_____

_____

_____

_____ [3]

62 Describe the Fetch Decode Execute Cycle in a computer system.

Fetch _____

_____

Decode _____

_____

Execute _____

_____ [3]

63 Explain the role of the following CPU Registers and Components:
PC, MAR, MDR, CIR, Accumulator, ALU, CU, Cache.

PC _____

MAR _____

MDR _____

CIR _____

Accumulator _____

ALU _____

CU _____

Cache _____ [8]

64   Write a Python program that uses a 1D array to store and
      manipulate data.

      _____

      _____

      _____

      _____

      _____

      _____

      _____

      _____

      _____

      _____

      _____   [5]

      _____

65   Write a Python program that uses a 2D array to store and output
      data.

      _____

      _____

      _____

      _____

      _____

      _____

      _____

      _____

      _____

      _____

      _____

      _____

      _____

      _____

      _____

      _____   [5]

      _____

┌───┐
│   │
│   Pause Point!   │
│   │
└───┘

Set 14

66 Write a Python program that uses subroutines to output a menu, then check that the user has chosen a valid option.

[5]

67 Explain the purpose of RAM in a computer system.

[2]

68 Describe the role of ROM in a computer system.

[2]

69 Explain how a control system with a microprocessor works.

_____

_____

_____

_____

_____

_____

_____   [3]

70 What are secondary storage devices? Give two examples.

_____

_____

_____

_____

_____

_____

_____   [3]

Pause Point!

The CPU is the brain of the computer. Knowing the components, registers & busses.

Flash cards are a great idea for this!

Set 15

71   Explain how analogue data is represented in a digital format.

_____

_____

_____

_____

_____

_____

_____   [3]

72   Explain the concept of positive and negative two's complement binary.

_____

_____

_____

_____

_____

_____

_____   [3]

73   What is virtual memory and why is it used?

_____

_____

_____

_____

_____

_____   [3]

Virtual memory is really helpful, but remember that using it regularly will slow your computer.

Increasing the size of the RAM is the solution for this.

74 The Fetch Decode Execute cycle is part of the Von Neumann
architecture. Describe the Fetch Decode Execute Cycle.

Fetch _____

_____

Decode _____

_____

Execute _____

_____ [3]

75 Explain how cloud storage works and some of the associated risks.

_____

_____

_____

_____

_____

_____

_____

_____

_____

_____ [5]

Pause Point!

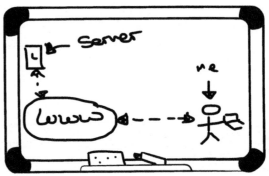

Set 16

76   Describe the roles of routers and switches in a local area network.

_____

_____

_____

_____

_____

_____

_____

_____

_____   [4]

77   Explain the differences between ethernet and fiber optic cables.

_____

_____

_____

_____

_____

_____   [3]

78   What is the purpose of RAM in a computer system?

_____

_____

_____

_____   [2]

79   What is the purpose of ROM in a computer system?

_____

_____

_____

_____   [2]

80 Explain the role of a microprocessor in a control system.

_____

_____

_____

_____

_____

_____

_____

_____   [3]

Pause Point!

When you look for revision resources, **"primary storage"** is often called "primary memory" or just "memory".

Set 17

81 Describe three types of secondary storage devices.
Include their characteristics and where you would recommend their use.

Storage Device 1: _____
_____
_____
_____

Storage Device 2: _____
_____
_____
_____

Storage Device 3: _____
_____
_____
_____ [9]

82 What is virtual memory and why is it used?

_____
_____
_____
_____
_____ [3]

83 Explain the concept of cloud storage and its advantages.

_____
_____
_____
_____
_____
_____ [3]

84   What is serial data transmission and where is it commonly used?

_____

_____

_____

_____

_____

_____

_____   [3]

85   Given the following, identify which are IP addresses and which are
        MAC addresses:
        A: 192.168.1.1
        B: 00:0a:95:9d:68:16
        C: 2001:0db8:85a3:0000:0000:8a2e:0370:7334
        D: 01-00-5E-00-00-FC.

A   [   ]

B   [   ]   You need to be able
                          to recognise both
C   [   ]   IPv4 **and** IPv6
                            addresses!

D   [   ]   [4]

Pause Point!

Set 18

86   Rewrite this pseudocode algorithm using a FOR loop.

```
B ← FALSE
INPUT Num
Counter ← 1
WHILE Counter <= 12 DO
   IF A[Counter] = Num THEN
      B ← TRUE
   ENDIF
   Counter ← Counter + 1
ENDWHILE
```

_____
_____
_____
_____
_____
_____
_____
_____
_____   [4]

87   Describe the main differences between IPv4 and IPv6.

_____
_____
_____
_____
_____
_____   [3]

When you use iteration, look for the variable that controls how many times the loop executes. FOR loops have a count controller built in.

88 A student has decided to keep their class work on a cloud storage account.

Discuss the advantages and disadvantages of them using cloud storage.

_____

_____

_____

_____

_____

_____

_____ [3]

89 A student attends an online lesson that uses duplex data transmission. Explain why a video call with their teacher requires duplex data transmission.

_____

_____

_____

_____

_____ [2]

90 What is a checksum and why is it used?

_____

_____

_____

_____

_____

_____

_____

_____ [4]

Pause Point!

Set 19

91   Rewrite this pseudocode algorithm using an IF-ELSE statement.

```
INPUT Num
IF Num > 10 THEN
    PRINT "Number is greater than 10"
ENDIF
IF Num <= 10 THEN
    PRINT "Number is less than or equal to 10"
ENDIF
```

[2]

92   What is the purpose of a function in a programming language?

[2]

93   What is the difference between a local and a global variable in a programming language?

[4]

94 Explain the difference between a FOR loop and a WHILE loop.
Include pseudocode examples as part of your explanation for each.

_____

_____

_____

_____

_____

_____

_____

_____

_____

_____   [4]

95 Write a pseudocode algorithm to find the name "Fred" in this array.

names ← ["Asif","Sarah", "Cait", "Fred", "Alina"]

_____

_____

_____

_____

_____

_____

_____

_____

_____

_____

_____   [5]

Pause Point!

Why so much programming?

Paper 2 usually has a long 15 mark question at the end, and practice is key to feeling ready for answering this!

Set 20

96 Write a pseudocode subroutine that takes an array of strings as input and prints each string in the array.

_____

_____

_____

_____

_____

_____

_____

_____

_____

_____

_____

_____   [5]

97 Write a pseudocode algorithm to calculate the sum of all numbers in this array.

Mynums ← [12,65,23,1,7,15]

_____

_____

_____

_____

_____

_____

_____

_____

_____

_____

_____

_____   [5]

When you're working with arrays, you can assume the first index is 0, unless the questions says otherwise.

(sometimes these will start at 1)

98 This section of program code asks for a user's age to be entered. Update the pseudocode to include a validation check to ensure the age entered is between 1 and 100.

INPUT "Enter your age: ", age

_____

_____

_____

_____

_____

_____

_____

_____

_____

_____ [4]

99 This section of program code asks for a user's email to be entered. Update the pseudocode to include a validation check to ensure the email entered contains an "@" symbol.

INPUT "Enter your email: ", email

_____

_____

_____

_____

_____

_____

_____

_____

_____

_____ [4]

Although you can use strings like an array in Python, accessing a single letter in pseudocode requires you to use SUBSTRING()

100 Write a pseudocode algorithm to count how many times the string "apple" appears in this array.

Fruit ← ["apple","pear","apple","pineapple","peach"]

_____

_____

_____

_____

_____

_____

_____

_____

_____

_____   [5]

Pause Point!

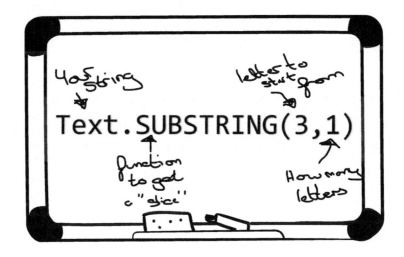

Set 21

101   A company is concerned about a ransomware attack.
Describe what is meant by a ransomware attack.

_____
_____
_____
_____
_____
_____
_____
_____   [4]

102   What is parallel data transmission and where is it commonly used?

_____
_____
_____
_____
_____
_____   [3]

103   What is a parity check and why is it used?

_____
_____
_____
_____   [2]

Do you feel like you're repeating questions?

That's because you are! Testing yourself on the same thing more than once helps you remember the best answer.

104   A part of a MAC address is given as 3F–A9–C2. Each pair of digits is stored as binary in an 8-bit register.

Complete the binary register for these pairs of digits.

3	F	A	9	C	2

_____
_____
_____
_____
_____
_____
_____   [3]

105   Negative denary numbers can also be represented as binary using two's complement.
Complete the binary register for the denary value –37.

You must show all your working.

_____
_____
_____
_____
_____
_____
_____
_____   [2]
_____

Pause Point!

Give Me MARKS!

When you're answering data representation questions, it's always a good idea to show your working!

Set 22

106   Explain the difference between an IP address and a MAC address.

_____
_____
_____
_____
_____
_____   [2]
_____

107   Compare the use of local storage and cloud storage.

_____
_____
_____
_____
_____
_____
_____
_____
_____   [4]
_____

108   A company is concerned about a worm attack. Describe what is
meant by a worm attack.

_____
_____
_____
_____
_____
_____
_____
_____   [4]
_____

There are over 150 technical terms in iGCSE Computer Science - if you're finding remembering these tough, try creating flashcards or Cornell Notes.

109   Identify the purpose of the algorithm below.

```
INPUT Num
IF Num MOD 2 = 0 THEN
    PRINT "Even"
ELSE
    PRINT "Odd"
ENDIF
```

_____
_____
_____
_____
_____
_____   [3]

110   What is the difference between a WHILE loop and a FOR loop?

_____
_____
_____
_____
_____   [2]

Pause Point!

Not all of the algorithms you see will be part of your "standard algorithms" - look for these first & name them if you can, then describe exactly what you see.

Set 23

111   Convert the hexadecimal number B3 to binary.

_____

_____

_____

_____

_____

_____ [2]

112   Evelyn has set a new tank for tropical frogs. The rocks that they bathe on must remain humid through a water spray built into the tank.

Describe how a control system could use sensors and a microprocessor to maintain a safe environment.

_____

_____

_____

_____

_____

_____

_____

_____

_____

_____

_____

_____ [6]

Questions about automation and control systems often follow a similar pattern:

INPUT -> PROCESS -> OUTPUT

113   What is half-duplex transmission and give an example of its use?

_____

_____

_____

_____

_____ [2]

114 Identify the purpose of the algorithm below:

```
INPUT Num
FOR Counter ← 1 TO Num DO
   PRINT Counter
NEXT Counter
```

_____

_____

_____

_____

_____

_____   [3]

115 Negative denary numbers can also be represented as binary using two's complement.

Calculate the 8 bit Two's Complement binary number for the denary value −33.

You must show all your working.

_____

_____

_____

_____

_____

_____   [2]

Pause Point!

Set 24

116 Negative denary numbers can also be represented as binary using two's complement.

Complete the binary calculation for the denary value −12.

You must show all your working.

_____

_____

_____

_____

_____

_____ [2]

117 Explain the roles of routers and switches in a network.

Router: _____

_____

Switch: _____

_____ [2]

118 Explain the process of sending data securely using asymmetric encryption.

_____

_____

_____

_____

_____

_____

_____

_____

_____

_____ [5]

119 Seth sees an email from his antivirus provider offering extra protection against spyware.

Describe what is meant by a spyware attack.

_____

_____

_____

_____

_____

_____

_____

_____ [4]

120 How can parity checks be used to spot errors in data transmission?

_____

_____

_____

_____

_____

_____ [2]

Pause Point!

Longer questions are often looking for your to apply your knowledge. Try using the technique below to structure your answer.

Point

Evidence

Explain

Set 25

121   Explain the purpose of virtual memory and how it works.

_____

_____

_____

_____

_____

_____   [3]

122   Explain simplex transmission and give an example of its use.

_____

_____

_____

_____   [2]

123   Alex reports a message to you that they think might be a phishing attempt.

Describe what is meant by a phishing attack.

_____

_____

_____

_____

_____

_____

_____   [4]

Real world attacks on our data happen in the milltions every day.

The website ThreatMap is a great resources to see this in real time.

124 Identify the purpose of the algorithm below.

```
INPUT Num
Sum ← 0
FOR Counter ← 1 TO Num DO
    Sum ← Sum + Counter
NEXT Counter
PRINT Sum
```

_____

_____

_____

_____

_____

_____ [3]

125 Convert the binary number 11010101 to hexadecimal.

_____

_____

_____

_____

_____

_____ [2]

Pause Point!

Binary & hexedecimal number in the exam can be up to 16 bits. Don't just preactice with 8 bit numbers!

Set 26

126 State one factor of authentication and describe an example of its use.

_____

_____

_____

_____

_____

_____ [3]

127 How can a checksum be used to spot errors in data transmission?

_____

_____

_____

_____

_____

_____ [2]

128 Convert the hexadecimal number 7E to binary.

_____

_____

_____

_____

_____

_____ [2]

129 What is the purpose of the IF statement in a programming language?

_____

_____

_____

_____ [1]

130 A server uses a central processing unit (CPU) to manage network resources. The CPU includes several components, such as the Current Instruction Register (CIR) and the Memory Data Register (MDR).

Explain how the CIR and the MDR are used in the fetch-decode-execute cycle.

_____

_____

_____

_____

_____

_____

_____

_____

_____

_____ [5]

```
Pause Point!
```

Some practice (and past paper) questions seem to repeat with a similar pattern. It's easy to forget to read these carefully - don't forget the questions *do* change!

Set 27

131   A student finds that their computer system is slowing down.
The student wants to use some utility software to help fix this issue.
Their friend has recommended a defragmenter.

Describe how defragmentation software will help improve the
performance of the computer.

_____

_____

_____

_____

_____

_____   [3]

132   Explain how data is stored and retrieved in a magnetic storage
device.

_____

_____

_____

_____

_____

_____   [3]

133   Explain the concept of two-factor authentication and provide an
example of its use.

_____

_____

_____

_____

_____

_____   [2]

Factors of Authentication are:

Something you **are**

Something you **know**

Something you **have**

134 Write an algorithm using pseudocode that shows how a checksum might be calculated.

Your algorithm should:
- Add the data together
- use integer division to divide by the number of data items
- concatenate the sum to the end of the original data

_____

_____

_____

_____

_____

_____

_____

_____

_____

_____

_____   [5]

135 Perform the binary addition of the following two numbers:

```
 10110011
+11010001
 _____
```

_____

_____

_____

_____

_____

_____   [3]

Pause Point!

Set 28

136 What is the purpose of a variable in a programming language?

_____
_____
_____
_____ [1]

137 Explain the main difference between high-level and low-level programming languages.

_____
_____
_____
_____
_____
_____
_____
_____ [4]

138 Explain how a firewall works and how it can help protect a computer system.

_____
_____
_____
_____
_____
_____
_____
_____ [4]

> The topics in Computer Science, aren't studied in isolation. Most questions will draw from several topics at once.
>
> Make sure you're reading the question carefully!

139 Describe how optical storage devices use lasers to store and read data.

_____

_____

_____

_____

_____

_____ [3]

140 Write a pseudocode algorithm that calculates the parity bit for a given 7-bit binary number. Your pasudocode should:

- take in a binary string
- calculate the correct parity bit for odd parity
- concatenate the parity bit to the start of the string
- return the updated binary bit pattern

_____

_____

_____

_____

_____

_____

_____

_____

_____

_____

_____

_____

_____

_____

_____

_____ [6]

Pause Point!

Set 29

141   A student finds that their computer system is slowing down. The student wants to use some utility software to help fix this issue. Their friend has recommended a disk cleanup utility.

Describe how disk cleanup software will help improve the performance of the computer.

_____

_____

_____

_____

_____

_____   [3]

142   What is meant by the term 'portability' in relation to high-level languages? Why is this considered an advantage?

_____

_____

_____

_____

_____

_____   [3]

Now that you're coming to the end of this set of practice questions, did you know that you can reuse them?

Go back over your original answers & try to improve them. How has your understanding changed?

143 Write a pseudocode algorithm that detects whether even parity has been used for a given 8-bit binary number.

Your code should:
- use a procedure to detect the parity
- take in a binary string
- output a suitable message for odd and even parity

_____

_____

_____

_____

_____

_____

_____

_____

_____

_____

_____

_____   [6]

144 What is biometric authentication and how does it work? Include an example in your answer.

_____

_____

_____

_____

_____

_____

_____

_____

_____

_____   [5]

145 Explain how solid-state storage devices use NAND or NOR
technology to store data.

_____

_____

_____

_____

_____

_____   [3]

_____

Pause Point!

```
FUNCTION AddOne(num)
    num ← num + 1
    RETURN num
END FUNCTION
```

By now, you should be comfortable placing your algorithms into subroutines.

As you move forward into the second part of the practice questions, you'll be using the same techniques combined into larger programs.

Set 30

146 What is the role of an operating system in handling interrupts?

_____
_____
_____
_____
_____
_____ [3]

147 Identify the purpose of the algorithm below.

```
INPUT Num
Factorial ← 1
FOR Counter ← 1 TO Num DO
    Factorial ← Factorial * Counter
NEXT Counter
PRINT Factorial
```

_____
_____
_____
_____
_____
_____ [3]

148 Why might a programmer choose to use a low-level language for a particular task, despite the complexity compared to high-level languages?

_____
_____
_____
_____
_____ [3]

Really think about what this question is asking you. How can you link it to what you've learnt about types of computer system?

149 Describe the role of antivirus software and why it is important for a computer system.

_____

_____

_____

_____

_____

_____ [3]

150 Write a pseudocode algorithm that calculates the colour depth given the number of unique colours that can be displayed.

Your algorithm should:
- pass the number of colours used into a function
- calculate the colour depth
- return the calculated colour depth

_____

_____

_____

_____

_____

_____

_____

_____

_____

_____ [4]

End Point!

Printed in Great Britain
by Amazon